Butterflies

NorthWord
Minnetonka, Minnesota

DEDICATION
For Iris and Emile
–M.S.

Photography © 2007:
Bob Jensen/Bruce Coleman Inc: cover; Shutterstock: back cover, pp. 4, 11, 12-13, 22, 24, 30, 32, 38, 39; Gail M. Shumway/
Bruce Coleman Inc: p. 5; Richard Shiell/Animals Animals–Earth Scenes: p. 7; Michael & Patricia Fogden: pp. 15, 26-27, 42;
Brian Kenney: pp. 16, 20, 21, 29, 34, 41; Frank Parker/Bruce Coleman Inc: p. 17; Kerry T. Givens/Bruce Coleman Inc: p. 25;
Harry N. Darrow/Bruce Coleman Inc: p. 31; Kim Taylor/Bruce Coleman Inc: pp. 36-37; Richard Szlemp: p. 43.

Illustrations by Andrew Recher
Designed by Laurie Fritsche
Edited by Kristen McCurry
Front cover image: Tiger swallowtails
Back cover image: Red admiral

NorthWord Books for Young Readers
11571 K-Tel Drive
Minnetonka, MN 55343
1-888-255-9989
www.tnkidsbooks.com

Library of Congress Cataloging-in-Publication Data

Stewart, Melissa.
     Butterflies / by Melissa Stewart ; illustrations by Andrew Recher.
          p. cm. – (Our wild world series)
     ISBN-13: 978-1-55971-966-7 (hardcover) – ISBN-13: 978-1-55971-967-4 (softcover)
     1. Butterflies—Juvenile literature. I. Recher, Andrew, ill. II. Title.

QL544.2.S745 2007
595.78'9--dc22
                                                    2006021916

Printed in Singapore

10 9 8 7 6 5 4 3 2 1

Butterflies

Melissa Stewart
Illustrations by Andrew Recher

NorthWord
Minnetonka, Minnesota

IF YOU ASK FRIENDS and family members to name their favorite insect, they will probably all say the same thing. "Butterfly." A butterfly's bright colors and large wings really catch our attention. We enjoy watching them flit and flutter among the flowers in our gardens.

Butterflies can also be found in fields, forests, wetlands, and deserts all over the world. They live on every continent except Antarctica.

Scientists have discovered and named more than 18,000 kinds, or species (SPEE-sees), of butterflies. Most species live in warm, tropical areas of the world, but more than 750 species make their homes in the United States and Canada.

From May to August, the blue copper butterfly can be seen flitting and fluttering in open forests and mountain meadows of the western U.S.

The giant swallowtail is most common in the southern U.S., but it can survive as far north as Canada and as far west as the Rocky Mountains.

Many butterflies are large and brightly colored, but some are small and blend in with their surroundings. The Queen Alexandra butterfly is as large as a robin. It lives in Southeast Asia and has an 11-inch (28-cm) wingspan. The pygmy blue butterfly is much smaller. It lives in the southern United States and is about the size of your thumbnail.

Butterflies
FUNFACT:

Butterflies and moths look similar, but there are three easy ways to tell them apart:

1. Butterflies are usually active during the day, while moths are usually active at night.
2. A butterfly's antennae (an-TEN-ee) have a round knob on the end, but a moth's antennae do not.
3. A butterfly perches with its wings spread out or held upright. A moth perches with its wings folded flat over its back.

The pygmy blue butterfly is small and blends in with its surroundings.
It usually lives in coastal areas and flies close to the ground.

whites & sulphurs

skippers

swallowtails

brush-footed

metalmarks

blues, coppers,
& hairstreaks

Butterfly Families

GROUP	EXAMPLES	DESCRIPTION
blues, coppers, & hairstreaks	eastern-tailed blue, gray hairstreak	small; bright red, blue, or orange wings
brush-footed	viceroy, mourning cloak, monarch, red admiral	medium to large; walk on four legs; small front legs are usually folded against bodies
metalmarks	swamp metalmark, little metalmark	small to medium; silvery bars or spots on wings
skippers*	long-tailed skipper, silver spotted skipper	small or medium; quick, darting movements; antennae end in a hook instead of a knob
swallowtails	tiger swallowtail, giant swallowtail	large; tails on back wings
whites & sulphurs	cabbage white, orange sulphur	small to medium; white, yellow, or orange wings

*Some scientists do not consider skippers to be butterflies. They put these little, darting insects in a group all by themselves.

An adult butterfly has six legs, four wings, and two antennae. Its body has three main parts: a head, a thorax, and an abdomen. The antennae on the top of a butterfly's small, round head have smelling sensors that help it find food and other butterflies. Below the antennae are two large, compound eyes. They see the world clearly and can sense even more colors than we can.

Between a butterfly's eyes is its proboscis (pro-BOS-kis), a long, thin tube that works like a drinking straw. Most of the time, a butterfly keeps its proboscis rolled up tightly. At mealtime, the insect uncoils its long tongue and slurps up sweet, sugary juices. Most butterflies feed on nectar, a sugary liquid made by flowers. Some butterfly species prefer to suck up tree sap or juices from rotting fruit.

A butterfly's legs and wings are attached to its thorax, or middle body part. Strong muscles inside the thorax power the insect's fluttering flight.

A butterfly's wings are covered with thousands of tiny, delicate scales. The scales overlap like the shingles on a roof, so they are waterproof.

A butterfly's abdomen contains its heart, a long, muscular tube that pumps blood. Breathing holes along the sides of the abdomen take in oxygen from the air. The breathing holes, or spiracles (SPEAR-ih-culs), are connected to a network of tubes that carry oxygen to all the different parts of the butterfly's body. The abdomen also contains body parts that digest a butterfly's food.

Butterflies
FUNFACT:

The scientific name for the group of insects that includes butterflies and moths is *Lepidoptera* (le-pih-DOP-ter-uh). It is the Latin word for "scaly wings."

This butterfly's proboscis is tightly coiled. When it is ready to feed, it will roll out its long, thin mouthparts and suck up sugary nectar.

When butterflies mate, the male releases a sperm packet into the female's body.
Some species mate several times a year, and others mate only once.

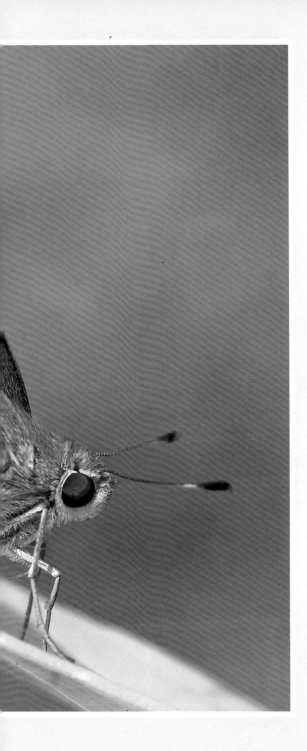

During certain times of the year, a female's abdomen is packed full of eggs. Before she can lay those eggs, the female must mate with a male butterfly. She releases strong-smelling chemicals (KEM-ih-culs) from her body to attract males. Using her antennae, she tries to pick up the trail of similar chemicals given off by male butterflies.

When a male and female find one another, they press the tips of their abdomens together. Then the male releases a sperm packet into the female's body. After the male leaves, the female butterfly is ready to begin laying eggs.

Female butterflies are careful to lay their eggs in places with plenty of food for their young. Most females lay tiny, greenish brown eggs one-by-one on the undersides of leaves, where predators (PRED-uh-torz) will not notice them. A few kinds of female butterflies lay large clusters of bright orange or yellow eggs. The shocking colors warn hungry enemies to stay away from the bad-tasting eggs.

Most females lay more than 100 eggs, and a few lay as many as 6,000. Even though butterfly eggs are colored to blend in with their surroundings or scare off predators, only two of every 100 eggs will hatch. Some are eaten, but many others are destroyed by heavy rains, drought (DROWT), wind, or disease.

Some butterfly eggs hatch in just a few days, but sometimes it takes a week, a month, or even longer for a developing butterfly to grow inside its egg. A few kinds of butterfly eggs are laid in the fall and do not hatch until the following spring.

When some young insects break out of their eggs, they look just like miniature, wingless versions of their parents. They are called nymphs (NIMFS). Other young insects look very different from the adults they will eventually become. They are called larva. The larva of a fly is known as a maggot, while young ants, beetles, and bees are called grubs. Caterpillars are the larvae (LAR-vee) of butterflies and moths.

This Pierid butterfly is laying eggs on a leaf. Many butterflies hide their eggs, but the bright yellow color of these eggs keeps them safe by warning predators that they taste bad.

This newly-hatched caterpillar is eating its shell.

When a butterfly caterpillar is ready to break out of its egg, the little larva uses its strong jaws and chewing mouthparts to chomp a hole in the hard, waxy shell. Then it wriggles, pushes, and pulls until it is free.

A caterpillar's main job is to eat and grow. Its first meal is usually its shell, which contains nutrients and energy. After devouring its shell, a caterpillar begins munching on the leaves, buds, or flowers of the plant it is on.

At first, a caterpillar's outer covering is soft and wet, but it quickly dries and hardens to form a tough exoskeleton. Like a suit of armor, the exoskeleton protects the insect's body. It also gives the caterpillar its shape and keeps the larva from drying out.

Butterflies
FUNFACT:

The word *caterpillar* comes from an Old French word that means "hairy cat." Long ago, people thought some species of caterpillars looked like tiny cats with long, spiky hairs.

The bodies of some caterpillars are covered with spikes, spines, or hairs that help keep them safe from predators.

Like an adult butterfly, a caterpillar's body consists of a head, a thorax, and an abdomen. A caterpillar does not have antennae on its head, but sense receptors (re-SEP-tors) all over its body taste, smell, and detect nearby movements. Even though a caterpillar may have as many as 12 eyes, it cannot see nearly as well as its parents. A caterpillar's simple eyes can sense light and dark, but they cannot form images.

A caterpillar does not have wings, but it does have six legs attached to its thorax. Each one ends in a claw that can be used to grasp leaves and other objects. Most caterpillars have 10 more leg-like structures on their abdomens. Unlike their six true legs, these 10 prolegs have suction (SUCK-shun) pads on the ends. They help a caterpillar anchor itself to leaves and stems.

Butterflies
FUNFACT:

Most caterpillars feed on plant material, but large blue butterfly caterpillars live in ant nests and devour young ant grubs.

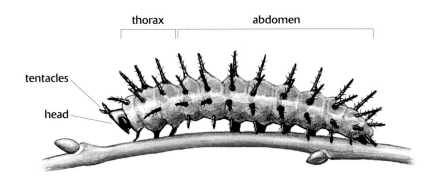

thorax

abdomen

tentacles

head

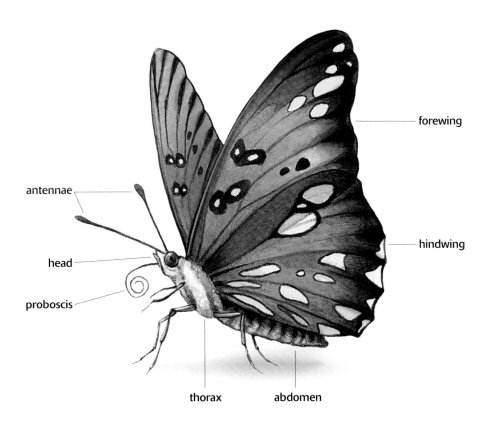

forewing

antennae

hindwing

head

proboscis

thorax

abdomen

When you look at a spicebush swallowtail caterpillar's false eyespots up close,
it is easy to see why these little larvae often fool birds into thinking they are snakes.

Even though caterpillars have lots of legs, they move slowly. That makes them easy targets for a wide variety of predators, including birds, toads, praying mantises, parasitic flies, wasps, mice, rats, opossums, and skunks. To stay safe, most caterpillars stay hidden under leaves as much as possible. Painted lady caterpillars and silver-spotted skipper caterpillars use silk that they make inside their bodies to build tent-like structures where they can eat in peace.

Because caterpillars cannot hide all the time, most have special body features to help them avoid enemies. Many caterpillars are green or brown, so they blend in with their surroundings. Viceroy and white admiral caterpillars look like bird droppings, so most predators do not pay much attention to them.

Monarch (MON-ark) and pipevine swallowtail caterpillars absorb poison from the foods they eat. The poison makes the caterpillars taste bad, so most predators spit them out. When a gray hairstreak caterpillar feels threatened, it can pull its head into its body. Common buckeye and red admiral caterpillars have spiky spines that make them look larger and more ferocious.

The more food a caterpillar eats, the faster it grows. When its insides press against its hard exoskeleton, the larva stops eating. It twists, squirms, and wriggles until its outer covering breaks open and then cracks all the way down its back.

When the larva emerges from its old exoskeleton, its new coat is still soft and moist. The caterpillar takes in extra air to stretch the flexible covering as much as possible. The insect rests until the exoskeleton hardens, and then it starts to eat again.

A wheel bug is one of the many predators cloudless sulphur caterpillars must try to avoid.

Soon after the Pilgrims landed in what is now Massachusetts, they noticed a beautiful golden ring around the chrysalis of a common North America butterfly. It reminded the Pilgrims of a king's crown, so they named the butterfly *monarch*.

Most butterflies spend one or two weeks in their caterpillar stage. During this time, they molt, or shed their exoskeleton, four or five times. When a caterpillar molts, its coloring may change, but its shape always remains the same.

Just before the final molt, most caterpillars attach themselves to a branch or twig with a bit of their silk. As a larva sheds its old coat, it becomes a pupa (PEW-puh). In butterflies, the pupa is the life stage between the crawling caterpillar and the adult with wings. The hard shell that surrounds a pupa is called a chrysalis (KRIS-a-lis). Because a pupa cannot move at all, its chrysalis must blend well with its surroundings. Some chrysalises are camouflaged (KAM-uh-flajd) to resemble bird droppings, while others look like berries or twigs.

During a butterfly's pupa stage, its body is stiff and rigid on the outside. But just below the surface, something incredible is happening. The insect's larval organs break down into a soupy liquid. Then they rearrange themselves to build adult body parts. In just a few days, weeks, or months, the fat, clumsy caterpillar transforms itself into a beautiful adult butterfly.

Shortly after a chrysalis splits open, an adult butterfly begins to emerge. First, it pushes its legs and antennae through the opening. Once the butterfly has a firm grasp on the outside of the chrysalis, it pulls the rest of its body out of the case and rests.

At first, the insect's body is wet and sticky. As it dries, the butterfly stretches and unfolds its crumpled wings. Then it pumps blood into the veins and spreads the wings wide until they dry and harden. After about 30 minutes, the butterfly is ready for its first flight. It takes off in search of its first sugary meal.

These butterflies have just broken out of their
chrysalises and are getting ready for their first flight.

Nearly all butterflies feed on nectar or other plant juices. To find flowers and other sources of food, butterflies use their excellent eyesight. They also rely on their antennae to smell food, and they use hair-like structures on their feet to taste it.

The length of a butterfly's proboscis determines which flowers it can feed on. If a butterfly has a short proboscis, it can only feed from flowers with easy-to-reach nectar. Butterflies with longer tongues can reach into deep flowers for their nectar.

Some butterflies get extra nutrition by sucking up salts in wet sand or muddy ground. They may also feed on animal droppings or dead animals.

Surprised to see a butterfly perching on the ground? Some butterflies feed on the salts in mud and sandy soil.

Wood nymph butterflies, which belong to the brush-footed family, live in Southeast Asia. Before these delicate butterflies mate, they "dance" around each other while in flight.

The energy a butterfly gets from its food helps it take in air, pump blood, and carry out many other body functions. Most importantly, it fuels the muscles that power flight. While many butterflies flit along at speeds of 5 to 10 miles (8 to 16 km) per hour, some fast-flying butterflies can cruise through the air at more than 30 miles (48 km) per hour.

Flying makes it easy for a butterfly to cross a large area of land quickly, so it can lay eggs in many different places. Flying also comes in handy when a butterfly is trying to escape from hungry spiders, toads, and lizards.

Butterflies
FUNFACT:

Because caterpillars and adult butterflies have different lifestyles and eat different foods, they do not compete with one another. This improves their chances of surviving.

Like caterpillars, adult butterflies have many enemies, including some that are expert fliers. To avoid or escape from dragonflies, praying mantises, and birds, butterflies have developed a wide variety of defenses.

Monarchs and pipevine swallowtail adults benefit from the poisonous plants they ate as caterpillars. The bad-tasting chemicals remain in the butterflies' bodies throughout their lives, offering constant protection. Viceroy butterflies do not taste bad, but they look so similar to monarchs that predators avoid them.

Zebra butterflies have a different kind of defense strategy. These large, beautiful insects don't taste bad, but they really stink. When zebra butterflies perch in large groups, their awful odor is enough to chase away even the hungriest predators.

The wings of many butterflies have shapes and patterns that help them blend in with their surroundings. A comma butterfly's wings look just like a leaf full of holes. When a question mark butterfly rests quietly on a tree trunk, the undersides of its wings blend perfectly with the bark. If a bird gets too close, the butterfly flashes the bright colors on the top of its wings and startles the predator away.

Butterflies
FUNFACT:

No one really knows the origin of the word *butterfly*. Some people think it comes from England, where many butterflies have buttery-yellow wings. Other people say it can be traced back to an old Dutch legend. The legend describes witches who turned themselves into little winged insects and stole butter and milk from farmers.

This question mark butterfly is hard to see as it perches among the leaf litter on a forest floor. The white marks in the middle of its wing give this insect its name.

Wood nymphs, pearly eyes, and common buckeyes have eyespots on the outer edges of their wings. These fake eyes sometimes fool hungry birds into nibbling a butterfly's wing instead of biting off its head. A butterfly can fly even if a little bit of its wing is missing, but no animal can survive without its head. An owl butterfly's eyespots are so large that they often scare predators into thinking the butterfly is a larger, more fierce animal.

The owl butterfly lives in the tropical forests of Central America. Most of the time, this butterfly is hard to see because it blends in with its surroundings. But even if a predator does spot an owl butterfly, it is usually scared off by the insect's large eyespots.

The Hessel's hairstreak butterfly lives in swamps along the East Coast of the United States. Both the caterpillar and the adult are green, which helps them blend in with their surroundings. If a predator gets too close, this butterfly can distract the attacker with its tail.

Hairstreak butterflies get their name from the thin, hair-like "tail" on their back wings. When an enemy gets too close, a hairstreak waves its tail. The attacker often goes after the tail, instead of more important body parts. Swallowtail butterflies can trick enemies in the same way.

Even if a butterfly can avoid all its enemies, it will not live very long. Most adult butterflies live just one or two weeks, and none can live more than a year. In North America, the longest-living butterflies are monarchs and mourning cloaks.

Monarchs are common throughout North America. Because they live longer than most other species of butterflies, they must be able to deal with cold, wintry weather. What do monarchs do when the temperature drops? They fly south, just like many birds.

Monarch butterflies can live up to six months. In places like Texas and Florida, monarchs have no trouble finding food and staying warm throughout their lives. Surviving is much more difficult in parts of the United States and Canada with long, cold winters.

Like all insects, butterflies are cold-blooded creatures. A butterfly's body temperature changes as the air temperature around it changes. On warm, sunny days, a butterfly's body is warm, too. Its muscles and brain have no trouble working. On cool days, a butterfly's body slows down. It has trouble moving and thinking.

Because a slow, sluggish butterfly is an easy target for hungry predators, monarchs have found a way to avoid cold winter weather. Like many birds, they fly to warmer parts of the world as autumn days grow cool.

Monarchs living in the eastern half of North America travel to south central Mexico, while monarchs living in the western half of North America migrate to southern California. Some monarchs fly up to 1,800 miles (2,900 km) to reach their winter homes.

Butterflies
FUNFACT:

On cool nights or rainy days, butterflies often hide under leaves or rocks. During this time, they rest, but they do not sleep the way people do. Butterflies do not have eyelids, so they can never close their eyes.

During their long migration, monarchs sometimes need to stop for a rest. Here you can see dozens of butterflies clustered together on a tree in Pismo Beach, California.

Even in Mexico and southern California, winter weather is not always warm. On cool or cloudy days, millions of butterflies blanket trees and rest. When the sun's warm rays heat up the air, huge flocks of monarchs take to the air in search of nectar-filled flowers.

In the spring, monarchs mate and begin the long journey north. Along the way, females stop here and there to lay their eggs. Migrating butterflies usually die before they reach their old summer homes, but when the eggs they laid develop into winged adults, they continue the northward journey. As a result, a new generation of monarchs spreads throughout the United States and Canada by midsummer.

Monarch butterflies can live a long time, but mourning cloaks can live even longer. If these large woodland butterflies are able to avoid their enemies, they may live up to 11 months.

Like monarchs, mourning cloaks have trouble surviving in cold weather. But instead of flying to warmer parts of the world, they hibernate. Like frogs, chipmunks, groundhogs, and many other animals, mourning cloaks spend the long, cold winter resting in a warm, cozy spot.

As the air temperature drops in autumn, a mourning cloak nestles inside a rotting log, a crack in a stone wall, or some other sheltered place. Safe from predators, the butterfly's brain, muscles, and other body parts gradually slow down. The mourning cloak produces chemicals that prevent its body from freezing solid.

As the spring sun warms the land, mourning cloaks come out of hiding. They drag their weak, sluggish bodies to the closest tree trunk and spread their wings wide. As the dark-colored scales on a mourning cloak's wings soak up the sun's heat, the butterfly's body warms up. To speed up the process, mourning cloaks shiver. The tiny movements their muscles make help spread heat throughout their bodies.

Butterflies
FUNFACT:

How did the mourning cloak get its name? The butterfly's dark wings reminded early American settlers of the cloak, or robe, worn by people mourning the death of a loved one.

With its wings spread wide, this mourning cloak is soaking up warm rays of sunlight. Soon its body will be warm enough to flit through the forest in search of tasty tree sap and rotting fruit.

A sulphur butterfly sips sugary nectar from a flower. Its feet resting on the flowers may pick up pollen grains, which the butterfly will spread to another plant. This helps seeds to grow.

A painted lady butterfly stops for a rest on an *Echinacea* flower. Many butterfly species like to feed on *Echinacea* nectar.

Because mourning cloaks spend most of their time in wooded areas, they eat a variety of foods. Besides nectar, they suck up tree sap, rotting fruit, and even juices in animal droppings. Because mourning cloaks spend less time sipping sugary nectar than monarchs, swallowtails, and checkerspots, they are not as important to plant reproduction.

As a butterfly feeds on flower nectar, its legs and proboscis may become dusted with powdery pollen. When the insect flutters to another blossom, some pollen may fall off the butterfly's body and land in the flower. Then the plant can use material in the pollen to make seeds, which will grow into new plants. Many plants could not survive without butterflies, bees, and other pollinators.

Even though adult butterflies help many plants reproduce, butterfly caterpillars spend most of their time gobbling up leaves, stems, and buds. Most people do not pay too much attention to caterpillars, but farmers do. The caterpillars of some butterflies can cause damage to important crop plants. Cabbage white caterpillars enjoy chowing down on cabbage, broccoli, and cauliflower. Giant swallowtail caterpillars, sometimes called orange dogs, feed greedily on the trees that grow lemons, limes, oranges, and grapefruits.

Since a butterfly's larval stage doesn't last long, caterpillars rarely do enough damage to kill the plants they feed on. As a result, both butterflies and flowering plants have been able to thrive on Earth for millions of years.

Butterflies
FUNFACT:

The first butterflies probably lived between 200 million and 300 million years ago. When flowering plants appeared about 130 million years ago, many new butterfly species developed. It did not take long for butterflies to spread to habitats all over the world.

Most caterpillars can eat only a few kinds of plants. Female butterflies are careful to lay their eggs on the plant species their caterpillars prefer. These black swallowtail caterpillars will only eat plants in the parsley family, which includes fennel, dill, carrot, celery, and Queen Anne's lace.

A gyas jewelmark belongs to the metalmark group and lives in the tropical forests of Central America and South America. When these forests are cut down or burned, the gyas jewelmark has trouble surviving.

Recently, however, some butterflies have begun to have trouble surviving. In some places, butterflies are losing their homes as fields and forests are destroyed to build houses, businesses, and parking lots. In other places, butterflies are starving because the plants they eat have been choked out by plants people have introduced. In still other places, butterflies are being harmed by chemicals.

In the United States, the U.S. Fish and Wildlife Services keep track of plant and animal species that are in danger of disappearing from Earth forever. At the time this book was written, 24 species of butterflies were included on the Endangered Species List.

The good news is that many people are working hard to save butterflies and protect the places where they live. Monarch butterflies have no trouble surviving in North America, but the monarchs that migrate to Mexico find less and less land to live on every winter. In some parts of Mexico, people have set aside natural areas for monarch butterflies. When tourists go to see Mexico's amazing monarchs, the money they spend helps people living in the area. Then they do not have to cut down trees to survive.

The rare Oregon silverspot is gaining population thanks to people who are allowing violets to grow in their yards, which is what the silverspot caterpillar eats.

It is too late to save Xerces blue butterflies, but there are many simple things you can do to help other butterflies survive far into the future.

The Xerces blue butterfly once lived along the West Coast of the United States, but it died out in the 1940s. Many other species of blue butterflies are also in trouble. Luckily, people are trying to help them. Near San Francisco, California, groups of adults and children have planted sunflowers and deerweed to help Palos Verdes blues. Near Albany, New York, people are protecting sandy areas where pine trees grow. It is the perfect habitat for Karner blue butterflies and the wild lupine plants their caterpillars feed on.

People are also working to save Schuas swallowtails, Mitchell's satyrs, and many other endangered butterfly species. To help the butterflies living in your area, you can plant a community butterfly garden. These special gardens, with plants like butterfly bushes, zinnias, hollyhocks, and sassafrases, are popping up in schoolyards and town parks all over North America. If butterflies have places to live and plants to feed on, they will continue to be part of our world far into the future.

Internet Sites

You can find out more interesting information about butterflies and lots of other wildlife by visiting these Internet sites.

www.projects.ex.ac.uk/bugclub/cater.html　　AmateurEntomologists/Raising Caterpillars

www.butterfliesandmoths.org/　　Butterflies and Moths of North America

http://butterflywebsite.com/　　The Butterfly Website

http://bsi.montana.edu/web/kidsbutterfly/　　The Children's Butterfly Site

www.enchantedlearning.com　　Enchanted Learning

www.fieldmuseum.org/butterfly/default.htm　　The Field Museum

www.monarchwatch.org　　Monarch Watch

www.smm.org/sln/monarchs/top.html　　Science Museum of Minnesota

Index

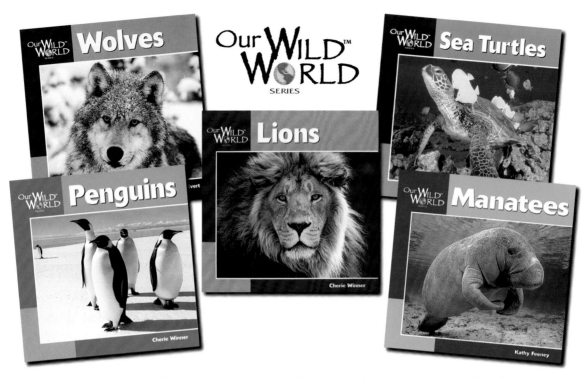

Titles available in the Our Wild World Series:

NorthWord
Minnetonka, Minnesota